A GOLF SWING YOU CAN TRUST

John Hoskison

Former European PGA Tour Player

PGA Cup v USA 1998-92

European PGA Team Championships 1992

Winner of the National PGA Professionals Grand Slam

British PGA Surrey Golf Association Captain

International Bestselling Author

SPO016000 Sports & Recreation, Golf

Book and Cover design by eBook Prep
www.ebookprep.com

February, 2017
ISBN: 978-1-61417-932-0

ePublishing Works!
www.epublishingworks.com

PRAISE FOR JOHN HOSKISON

"I first went to see John 5 years ago for the usual stuff: head in hands, not knowing what shot was coming next! John kept it simple and got me enjoying golf again. I can't recommend him enough."
~Mick Fitzgerald,
TV Sports Presenter - Former National Hunt Jockey

"When the rest of us were trying to squeeze one out there, John Hoskison would step up and blast it down the middle as if no trouble existed."
~Pete Oakley
2004 British Senior Open Champion

"John taught himself a great technique and knows as much about the golf swing as anyone I've met."
~Nick Mitchell,
Former European Tour PGA Player

"John has solid orthodox technique and is a great student of the game. He always told me 'simple is best'".
~Andrew Murray,
European PGA Tour
1989 European Open Champion

CONTENTS

FOREWORD

John Hoskison has been a member of the European PGA Tour and represented Europe against the USA in PGA Cup matches. Regarded as one of the straightest hitters in the game, John built his swing on the guidelines set down in this book.

INTRODUCTION

If you want to improve your golf swing, but no matter what you try you don't hit the ball better, then read this introduction. It explains the reason most golfers fail to see results when they have lessons or try out tips from magazines. If you want to hit the ball more consistently then knuckle down for five minutes and read the following story about how I learned a very important lesson that is relevant to beginners and tour pros.

When I was fourteen I was a pretty good golfer playing off a handicap of four, but I had a fault in my swing that made the ball curve from left to right in flight. I hit most fairways but in a left to right wind my fade became a slice and I didn't hit the ball far enough if I wanted to go to the next level. My father, who had taught me from a young age, wasn't experienced enough to spot my swing fault and fixed up for me to have a lesson from the best teacher in Europe—John Jacobs—'Doctor Golf' himself.

The morning we drove to Sandown Park Golf Club, where John Jacobs was the resident teaching pro, I was really nervous. I remember carrying my clubs to the teaching bay, head held high, chest puffed out, and shaking hands with the man who taught half the Ryder Cup squad.

Even though my knees were trembling, when I started hitting balls they flew down the practice range exactly the same way they did on the course—a slight fade from left to right. I hoped it wasn't a serious fault and was thrilled when John Jacobs announced he had diagnosed the problem and it only needed a slight change to cure my fade.

John Jacobs pointed out that the ball was too far forward in my stance which meant my shoulders were open and my head was set at the wrong angle. My incorrect stance made me take the club back on the outside, which was the fundamental cause of me cutting across the ball. To cure my fault John Jacobs simply moved the ball back in my stance and tweaked my shoulders and head to the right. 'Now hit some balls from this position' he said.

In the matter of a few minutes John Jacobs had changed the line of my swing. From my new position I automatically took the club back on a better path and without having to make any other changes I started to approach the ball on the right line. And the proof was there for all to see. When we went to hit balls off the grass my divots were straight—not pointing left as they normally did. Instead of the ball taking off to the left it was starting out slightly right of target! Fantastic! I had cracked golf and it was so damned simple—I couldn't wait to go out onto the course and break my course record!

And so to Effingham Golf Club that very afternoon. I clearly remember teeing it up on the first hole full of expectation, ready to see my new power draw rip down the middle. I made sure my ball position was correct, my shoulders square and my head tilted at the correct angle. Sure it all felt a bit weird but what the heck! Even the strike with my driver felt better but as I looked up expecting to see the ball curve from right to left it started off right and then sliced off even more. When the ball landed it took one bounce and shot straight out of bounds. I hit another—same result. I tried it off the second tee but after losing three balls in two holes I never tried the changes again. The diagnosis had to be wrong.

You won't believe how hard I worked for the next ten years. My hands bled through hitting thousands of balls and I investigated every possible theory to rid myself of the fade that plagued me. I tried the upright swing of Jack Nicklaus, the distinctive rhythm of Tom

Watson's swing and even the flatish action of
Ben Hogan. But no matter what I tried my weak
left to right flight stayed. The one thing I never
investigated again was my address position.

However, through sheer hard work on the
short Surrey courses I made myself into a scratch
golfer and lured by the possibility of fame and
fortune I turned pro. I even managed to win
myself a card to play the European Tour. But
when I needed to step up a gear, off the back tees
on long tournament courses I failed abysmally —
Royal Birkdale being a case in point. The stiff
Lancashire breeze turned my fade into a
whopping great slice and I finished last in the
PGA Championships, which Nick Faldo went
onto win.

In 1985 I almost gave up golf. On the advice
from a friend I took a job selling life insurance
but found out pretty quickly that extracting a
monthly premium from potential customers was
harder than getting a buried ball out of 'Hells
Bunker'. With no money coming in and that year
the PGA Championships taking place at
Wentworth I decided to have one last try.

I played with Sandy Lyle in practise — not a
great idea when suffering from a lack of
confidence, and the night before the first round I
lay awake desperately trying to work out which
swing would get me round the next day. What
could I try — I'd tried everything and I didn't
want to just chop my way round the course. So

searching for an answer I went right back to the start—to my lesson with John Jacobs. He'd seemed so sure the answer was simple. And then finally it hit me.

My lesson with John Jacobs had changed the line of my swing but not my hand action. Coming into the ball on a new line my hands were confused. They had to be given time to develop a new release at impact and I hadn't given them the opportunity. The inescapable truth I learned that night is that change takes time. There is an inevitable process one has to go through when changing a swing and unless you're tough enough to be patient while the process takes place you will ultimately fail.

Before the first round of the PGA Championships I practised the stance John Jacobs had given me. With years of experience behind me I was able to rehearse the necessary hand action to make the action work.

I'm not kidding when I tell you I almost wept when I saw my first tee shot drill down the middle and then curve slightly to the left. I made the cut that week, earned a good cheque and with regards to striking the ball I have never looked back. Shortly after the event I won the first 'Shooting Star' award for most improved order of merit position and shortly after I went on to win the PGA National Club Professional Championships. With my new found ability to square up the blade in 1991 I returned to my nemesis and played all four rounds in the Open Championship at Royal Birkdale shooting 71 on the final day. Even in a strong left to right wind I had learned to draw the ball.

If you slice or hook and you want to change how you swing, there is no alternative but to improve your swing path into the ball. That is relatively easy. But for you to persevere through the inevitable process of change it is vital you understand the logic behind the alterations. Only then will you have the nerve and patience to stick with them.

It is highly unlikely if you change your swing path you will hit the ball better immediately. If you've played golf for some time your hands probably know only one way to release the club, just as mine did when I went for my lesson with John Jacobs. But if you stay patient the advice in this book offers you a real chance to become a better golfer and make a fundamental change to your golf swing that you've never managed before.

A GOLF SWING
YOU CAN TRUST

Welcome to the rest of the book—if you follow the logical progression of lessons you will improve. But before we take a look at the swing in detail and how to change it, let's take a look at the golf swing in general and the overall object of the book.

The golf swing is basically divided into two parts—the backswing and downswing. If a golfer makes a good backswing the downswing becomes pretty simple. But a bad backswing, with the club in the wrong position, means the golfer has to make complicated adjustments on the downswing which limit power and accuracy.

Building a good backswing and improving the line of your swing is our number one priority. Once we have achieved that, it's a question of keeping up the changes while the rest of your swing, particularly your hand action, adapts to your new improved swing path into the ball.

Before we can start constructing the backswing we have to understand it. It's easy to do that because the golf swing is a chain reaction of moves and we can trace it from the top of the backswing right back to the start. It's there we find the nucleus of a good swing and the secret of changing the line.

It may not come as a great surprise that aim and grip ultimately define the quality of the backswing. Aim poorly or grip the club incorrectly and it affects the takeaway, the plane of the swing and eventually the position of the club when it reaches the top. But nearly all golf books tell you this yet very few golfers ever learn to stand correctly to the ball. Therefore something has to be wrong with the way this message is communicated.

So I'm going to try something different. I'm going to describe the chain reaction of the swing in an unusual way hoping the words give you a new understanding of how the grip and alignment directly affect the shape of the swing.

Following is a hypothetical conversation between the two main components of the backswing—the hands and the body. During any golf swing—even the swing of a top pro, the hands and body are in constant communication with each other trying to work out how to get the club back to the ball.

The scene is set with a golfer, who we'll call Pete, an habitual slicer, standing on the tee ready to hit. As Pete makes his final preparations to start the swing his hands and body start to talk to each other.

Body: Morning guys — how you feeling?

Hands: Bit trembly — late night last night.

Body: How's the club face aiming?

Hands: Ten yards left.

Body: Not as much as the shoulders then. Hope he doesn't try that one piece takeaway the pro taught him. He'll go straight on the outside. You better get ready to take over.

Hands: We should go on strike!

Body: You did last week remember — three lost balls and two tiles off the roof of the manager's house. Thought the pro told him to get his left hand round more — help him square up the shoulders.

Hands: He's forgotten that bit.

Body: Oh well — hope you're ready to work hard — speak in a moment when he starts the backswing. Catch up with you later.

Hands: You'd better or it's another lost ball.

Pete starts the backswing trying his new one piece takeaway but with a weak grip, the club aiming left and the shoulders even further

*left, a good takeaway is impossible. To avoid
swinging on the outside the hands take over
and quickly roll the club back onto the inside.*

Body: Wow—got your breath back? What happened to smooth and slow. You guys okay?

Hands: He went for the one piece takeaway, club went miles outside. We had to take over and roll it back. Boy, it must have looked ugly! We could've made a better job of it but he's swinging so fast we've overdone it—the club's travelling round his arse. You've gotta help us!

Body: Not Again? All that effort so early in the morning. We'll heave the club onto a steeper plane. Here goes.....

*In an effort to move the club onto a more
upright swing path the body stops turning
and goes into a massive reverse pivot where,
with no space to swing, the left arm impacts
against the chest and crumbles.*

Body: Woah! Overdid that one—that hurt. Have to pay another visit to doc.

Hands: If he swung a bit slower he'd give us half a chance. We're in real trouble now. One minute we were aiming left. With overswing the club's pointing twenty yards right.

Body: Want me to try to swing round and get

him back on track? Might give you less to do.

Hands: Give it a go.

To try to realign the downswing onto the correct path the shoulders swing round but Pete's swinging so fast the club is thrown onto the outside in a classic 'over the top' move. In a last ditch bid to save the shot from disaster the body tells the hands it's 'battle stations'. Rather like the SAS the hands are relied on in times of real trouble.

Body: Sorry guys, nothing I could do—he's not heard the Golden Bear's advice 'swing slow from the top'. We're coming at the ball miles from the outside. You'd better hold the face open or he'll hit that house again.

Hands: Hold the face open, *that's all we ever do!*

Coming into impact the hands desperately try to hold the clubface open to stop the ball going left. The driver comes in steep jarring into the ground. The ball takes off left cutting back in a horrible slicing arc. As the hands and body check for injury they hear Pete comment.

Pete: Maybe the pro got it wrong about the takeaway—that's the worst slice I've hit in ages. Think I'll try turning my hips faster from the top—that may stop my slice!

Okay that was a bit of fun, but hopefully you get the drift. The correct stance is vital if you want to build a simple swing that repeats. But most golfers switch off and skip these chapters of a golf instruction book. I understand that. The grip and aim are not as alluring as advice on the theoretical advantages of pronation or supination through impact. And hey! You've been told you have a nice practise swing — you can't be *that* far off. Aiming correctly is for beginners!

So just to dispel any reservations you may have that this book is not for you, here's one last piece of motivational talk before we move on to check your stance. It's very often a golfer makes a great practise swing but when they come to hit the ball the swing's completely different. That's because the hands and body don't communicate on a practise swing — they let you get on with it on your own. They only bother to 'talk' to each other when you're about to hit a shot at a specific target.

When the crunch comes and you're ready to swing back, if the aim of the club doesn't match up to your intended swing path, they hit the panic button, take control and stick the swing on autopilot. They programme in what they have to do and you can't override it. You might try to take the club back in one piece but it you're not aiming correctly — they quickly take over. And if you think you can kid them you'd have done it by now.

If you are aiming at a target 250 yards away and your clubface is only 3 degrees to the right, it will be pointing 13 yards right of target. If you try to replicate your nice square practise swing, but your hands pick up where the club is aiming the two angles are so conflicting your orthodox swing becomes impossible.

The only time you can override your natural alarm system is when you're standing in front of a pro and he's watching you like a hawk. Then the alarm system becomes dormant—it trusts the pro to watch over you. Soon as you walk out the teaching bay, it switches back on.

There's no escaping the simple truth that if you want to hit the ball better, first you have to improve the line of your swing—cut and dried. To do that you have to make sure you stand correctly to the ball. That means taking good aim with the body *and* the club. Even the great Jack Nicklaus used to check his aim and stance regularly!

Stay with me on this one. Let me walk you through this book and explain how to change your swing. Follow my advice to build a swing you can trust, then I'm sure if you ask them nicely, your hands will let you take over the controls.

LESSON 1
CLUB HEAD AIM

In my example of Pete hitting a ball, we've seen how the aim of the clubface has a direct influence on the swing path of the backswing.

If the club face is aiming left of target or 'closed' a golfer has two options. They can either take the club back at right angles to the club face, which would mean a swing path on the outside. Or in most cases, just as Pete does in my example, the hands quickly take over and try to compensate for the poor aim by rolling the club onto the inside. This results is a swing plane that would end up too flat without a massive adjustment.

In the opposite case, where someone has the club face 'open' at address, a golfer will likely sweep the club back on the inside, but in this version of the swing the arms move too close to the body. When the left arm has no more space to swing, it lifts up almost vertically. This leads to a weak narrow 'lifted' backswing that is too steep.

Both these takeaways mean the golfer has to make complicated adjustments during the swing to try to get back to the ball in a reasonable position. Sorting out a 'loop' requires phenomenal timing and the reason why many golfers hit good shots followed by disastrous ones.

The simplest swing to repeat is one that travels roughly up and down on the same line or 'plane', requiring the minimum of adjustments. In order to build a swing that repeats you must aim correctly. If you are in any doubt about being able to aim correctly when you take up your stance try the following tip.

Tip to Get Club Face Correct

The best way to ensure the clubface is aiming correctly is to draw a line on the ball and point it at your intended target. All you have to do then

is adjust the face so it's positioned at right angles to the line. This is allowed on the greens when putting and on all tee shots even in competition.

Rather than aiming the club at a

distant target, it is much easier to line up the clubface to a line on the ball. Once you have synchronised the two don't let the face change when you glance up at the target in preparation for the shot. Trust the new alignment even if it appears wrong. Your eyes will quickly adapt and a square club will soon look correct. Only then will it start to have a positive effect on the takeaway path.

Remember my lesson with John Jacobs. I didn't give my new stance long enough to work — don't make the same mistake. Regularly check you are not slipping back to old habits. The danger is that you may not bother with this simple tip, but whether you decide to try this tip or not, it is crucial to check whether you are aiming accurately at the target.

LESSON 2
THE IMPORTANCE OF THE GRIP

I've got some friends who are builders where I teach—tough guys—great fun. I've seen them at work and I marvel at the meticulous way they set the first line of bricks when they build a wall. They tell me it's all about preparation. Yet when they set up to hit a golf ball nothing is lined up correctly—they just want to smash hell out it.

It took me ages to convince them that getting the aim and grip correct are as important as setting the first line of bricks when they build a wall. Eventually they 'got it' and have never looked back. In the following paragraphs I'm going to explain why the grip is so important—I hope you 'get it' too.

Once the clubface is set square the next stage to building a good backswing is making sure you grip the club correctly. Most golfers know the grip's important—you might have already made adjustments to it during lessons. But it's rarely pointed out the devastating side effects of a bad grip, and you need to know this or you may not take the time to make important adjustments.

Irrespective of how you place your hands on the club, your grip must allow your arms to hang down correctly. Most golfers know the feet, hips and shoulders have to aim at the target—that's not news. But what you might not have heard before is how important it is to have the arms also in the correct position. A line drawn across them, about two inches below the elbows must point at the target—and it's your grip that determines whether you get this right. To check whether your grip needs adjusting try the following test.

Grip Check

Take up your stance over a ball. When you have finished lift up your arms in front of you to shoulder height. There are two important characteristics to check. Firstly, the leading edge of the clubface must be vertical. That means the club is square to your body and can work in harmony with it throughout the swing.

Then look at your arms, about two inches below your elbows (towards your wrists). A line drawn across them at this point must be horizontal. Imagine if I walked across with a club and tried to balance it across your arms. Would it stay there or would it fall off? If it would fall off to the left you are setting up for a slice. Your left arm would be lower than the right, which would almost definitely mean your shoulders are open  at address. If it would fall off to the right it would mean you are setting up for a hook.

There is one important thing to remember when you carry out this test. If your arms are straight out in front of you (horizontal) the club shaft will be at an upward angle to your arms. The same angle it was relative to your arms in the address position. Because of this angle the first point your arms can be level is about two inches below your elbows.

If the club would fall off to the left, to get the arms level, you might need to make several adjustments. You might have to drop your right shoulder slightly—it should be lower than your left. In addition you might need to raise your left forearm slightly and turn your left hand round clockwise into a 'stronger grip'. It will probably take some experimentation to get it right, but before you finish make sure you could balance a club across your arms. If I think back at the hundreds of golfers I've taught who've sliced the ball, nine out of ten have had their left arm too low when they try this test.

In the opposite scenario, if the club would fall off to the right you have to make the corresponding alterations. When you've carried out the adjustments and lower the club back into the address position, make sure that if a golfer looked at you from behind, a line across your forearms, just below your elbows, points directly at the target.

If you want to build a swing you can trust nothing you learn will be as important as this. The way your arms hang at address directly influences the quality of the takeaway. It doesn't matter if you stand to the ball with the posture of a top pro, if your arms aren't level you cannot take the club back in a co-ordinated move with the body, hands and arms working together and your swing will become a series of complicated adjustments. If you've got time to hit 500 balls a day and some real core talent, you could develop your timing to handle the inevitable 'loop' that this fault creates. But if you don't have extraordinary ability — get this wrong and your swing is pretty much doomed

There's a lot of good information in this book, but if I had to single out the most important piece — this is it. This tip is the golden nugget, the buried treasure you've been searching for. This is as important as the advice John Jacobs gave to me, which I dismissed after a few shots. If you want to waste endless hours on the practice ground as I did, or needlessly buy clubs and spend huge amounts on tuition then ignore this advice. But if you want to build a solid swing you *have* to get this right. How your arms hang at address directly influences the next part of the swing, the takeaway, which we will be discussing in the next chapter.

Well done so far — let's go get a coffee.

Taking Stock — Coffee Break

Before I explain how to take the club back correctly I want to give you a rough understanding of where you are now with better clubface aim and the correct position of the arms. If you've managed to alter these aspects of the swing and synchronise your stance you've done really well. But getting only these two things right won't necessarily mean you hit the ball any better — yet. The grip and stance were only part of the puzzle. But to help keep you positive, following is an explanation of why things will become easier.

Imagine I gave you a full glass of water and asked you to place it in the middle of a table cloth which is lying on a table. No problem you think. You walk across to the table with the glass, but instead of finding the table cloth neatly draped over the table, the thing is scrunched up in a mess. You try to balance the glass in the middle but of course it tips over immediately. Before you try it again you have to smooth out the cloth — a bit like sorting out your swing.

So first you get hold of one corner and pull it gently towards you. Effectively that's what we've done sorting out your clubface and grip. But what would happen if you tried to balance the glass of water again without any more changes. You've only straightened out one corner. The middle of the cloth is still in a mess. If you tried balancing the glass again it would tip over. You need to straighten out another corner before you have a chance of the glass staying upright.

With that analogy in mind it's now time to make another adjustment to your swing that will allow you to start hitting better shots. It's now time to discuss the takeaway.

LESSON 3
YOU CAN'T BEAT A GOOD TAKEAWAY

The takeaway only lasts for about two feet but the small move goes a long way in defining the overall shape of the backswing. Because the golf swing is a chain reaction, from just a small movement away from the ball a good teacher will likely know where the club will finish up at the top of the backswing.

To explain that, imagine if I looked at a distant planet and recorded its journey through the sky for ten minutes. If I put that information on a computer I could calculate exactly where the planet would be in a hundred years time. Taking that logic to the golf swing, the path of the club, in the first couple of feet away from the ball, determines the overall shape of the backswing. If we can sort you out a good takeaway it will help shoot your club towards a great position at the top.

What Constitutes a Good Takeaway?

A good takeaway is one where the body, arms and hands, sweep the club away in a smooth coordinated move creating maximum width of arc

for power and accuracy. This is often referred to as a one-piece-takeaway. The problem is if you've gripped the club incorrectly in the past or aimed the club poorly your takeaway will have been wrong. Now you must re-educate the muscles to groove the correct move. Here are several drills to help.

One Piece Takeaway Exercise

Stand in your address position, then slide the club through your fingers until the butt of the club actually touches your body. If you're wearing a belt, the end of the club should pretty much rest against the buckle.

To practise the correct one piece takeaway simply turn the body so the unit of the body arms and club you've created (like a little triangle), stay in the same relative position. Just turn the shoulders and keep the club touching the belt buckle. Only move the club back a couple of feet maximum—this is where most people go wrong.

Don't go back too far!

Learn to turn back and forward keeping the unit together. Don't worry if it feels wooden and robotic—it's meant to. But even though it feels rigid try to get some rhythm in the move—back and forward—back and forward—until you can do it with the monotony of a pendulum.

This turning motion of the body back and forward is not just confined to the golf swing. It happens all the time in everyday life. Following is just one of many examples I use to describe the 'feel 'of the correct takeaway, and the bottom half of the swing.

Imagine if a building caught fire but there were no firemen around—just a tank of water outside in the street. Together with your friends you'd stand in a line and pass buckets of water to one another. You've probably seen something like this in a film. One turns to his friend, gets the bucket, and turns round to pass it on. Back and forward they go, turning round and turning back—turning round and turning back. They don't just use their hands and arms, their whole body turns in a one piece move. This is what a good takeaway feels like—everything turning together. The only difference between the example and the swing is that in the swing you keep your head still.

When you have the feel of this pendulum move, try lowering the club down into its normal position and hitting a few very small shots at a target no more than fifteen yards away. This is a crucial exercise to practise. Keep the arms firm and don't use the hands. Best bet is to hit the shots off a small tee to make it as easy as possible. This is an exercise to develop a new line of swing not hit powerful shots into the distance so keep it slow and smooth. Effectively it's a chip shot and if you turn back and forward keeping your head still the ball should go dead straight, every time.

With regards to developing new hand action that matches your improved line into the ball, this is the first time you can start to re-educate your hands. If you carry out this small pendulum exercise correctly you are guaranteed to bring the club into the ball on the right path. But you might find the ball still travels slightly right or left. This shows how your hands currently work relative to the swing path.

If you normally hit with a slice or a hook it means your swing line has been aiming in one direction and your clubface pointing in another. If you can learn to hit the balls directly at the target, even though it's a very small shot, it means your hands and arms will be getting used to squaring up the blade to the swing path.

After years of watching my pupils practise this exercise I know the incredible benefits it offers. If I had practised it for a couple of days after my lesson with John Jacobs, I may well not have hit the first ball out of bounds and would have gone on to trust the alterations to my stance.

Using the Takeaway in a Full Swing

This exercise is to help you incorporate your new one piece takeaway into some full practise swings. Now we have synchronised the aim and swing path — practise swings become very important. Get into your address position but before you swing, bend down and put a ball directly behind the club head, rather than in front of it where the ball should be.

Take up your stance again, make sure the club is aimed correctly, then swing to the top of the backswing making sure you start the swing off with a one piece takeaway. As you do so, the ball will be sent rolling away. To see if you're taking the club back on a good path, all you have to do is look at where the ball has rolled.

With a good takeaway the ball will have rolled slightly behind you, reflecting the inside nature of the swing path created by the body turning. If however the ball rolls either straight back or worse, onto the outside, you know you have taken the club back too straight or outside the line.

This exercise not only indicates the initial swing path of the club, but it also helps a golfer to feel how smooth the takeaway should be. There's an old saying that the start of the swing should feel as though you are using the club to sweep leaves off the ground. The only way to do that is to have smooth one piece takeaway.

Two Club Takeaway Exercise

You may well have looked at junior golfers swinging the club and marvelled at how simple they make it look. And they are amazing. Give them a half decent grip and shortly after they start swinging the club on line, in plane, just like a pro. But it's not because they have more talent than an adult, normally it's because the club is slightly too heavy for them.

With a club that is slightly too heavy a junior golfer will create the necessary leverage to swing the club by using the body. Instinctively they use their most powerful muscles to inject momentum into the swing and naturally gravitate to a 'one piece takeaway.' But give a club to an adult, with stronger hands and arms and there is a tendency to override the natural way momentum should be created. Very often they start the swing off with hand action.

Try this exercise to help start the swing using a natural one-piece takeaway. Instead of warming up by swinging one club, put two together and from a normal stance make a swing. The extra weight will help you sweep the club away using your body to create the swinging motion. Practise with two clubs to promote a natural swing just like a junior.

Lunch and a Pep Talk

Time for a quick motivation talk. If you've stuck with this so far and have altered the club face, the grip and have practised a one piece takeaway then kudos to you. You have taken a massive leap forward in building a better swing. You might even have started to see some results, especially if you have hit a few gentle chips shots with the pendulum exercise. But that puts you in real danger of not completing the rest of this book and being over confident can be a dangerous thing. So here is an explanation of where you are right now.

Imagine you go to the doctor feeling unwell and he prescribes a course of penicillin tablets. We all know what he says as you walk out the door. 'Make sure you finish the course!' The question is what happens if you don't. Well it's not good news. Just as the bugs you're trying to kill are on the point of extermination, you stop taking the tablets and the bugs recover. Worse, they get stronger — they become super bugs. If you constantly tinker with your golf swing and keep trying out different theories to solve a swing problem, the fault you're trying to cure builds up immunity and it becomes harder to get rid of it each time you try.

You've done great if you've made the changes so far discussed in this book — now is the time to keep going. Make sure you finish the course!

LESSON 4
THE WRIST HINGE

Y ou've now learned to take the club away correctly so continuing the swing to the top will be easier than in the past. There's no need to describe the backswing inch by inch, as I would have to if someone was trying to get back on track after a bad takeaway, you just have to keep the swing going.

With the club now travelling at a smooth pace, enough momentum should have been built up for centrifugal force to automatically hinge the wrists. The only thing that stops the wrists cocking naturally is if the right leg buckles and weight is thrown onto the outside of the foot. The right leg needs to be anchored, offering a degree of resistance, for centrifugal force to kick in.

This can easily be achieved before you start swinging. When you take up your stance make sure you don't stand all limp and floppy like a rag doll. Imagine if I came along and tried to push you over. Your legs should be set firm enough to resist. If your legs were all floppy you'd lose balance and fall over. It's very important you don't over react to this advice though and keep your legs rigid. They have to react to the hips turning—just try to keep the right leg relatively firm.

The wrist hinge is a result of centrifugal force kicking in and is an important move in the golf swing. It defines the 'plane' of the swing. The

move sets up a new line for the arms to swing on and it's important they do. Instead of continuing round with the body, as they were during the one piece takeaway, in an orthodox traditional swing they start travelling on a more upright angle and it's the wrist cock that creates this new 'plane'. As a guide line, when the wrists have fully cocked, the butt of the club should be pointing roughly towards the ball.

Once the wrist cock has been completed you're

in what we call the half way back position and it's very important to hit balls with this half swing. It's like hitting a pitch shot from maybe forty yards off the green. While you're building up your new swing to full power, hitting shots from different swing lengths quickly develops your overall co-ordination and it's much easier grooving new habits when you're not operating at full speed.

There are two important things to remember when practising the half swing. Firstly, the two halves of the swing should always balance — the backswing and follow through are reflections of each other. When practising smaller shots the club should be swung back and through the same distance.

Secondly, just as the butt of the club pointed at the ball after the wrist cock on the backswing — a mirror image of that position should occur on the follow through. When you finish the half swing, the butt of the club should be pointing back at where the ball was. If a ball did happen to be on the tee, theoretically you should be able to hit a pitch shot back the other way.

Once you have learned to hinge the wrists correctly there is only one thing that can cause problems as you swing to the top. If the body gets lazy and the shoulders stop turning, you could still be in trouble. Making sure you complete a good shoulder turn is vital — but for some that can be a problem.

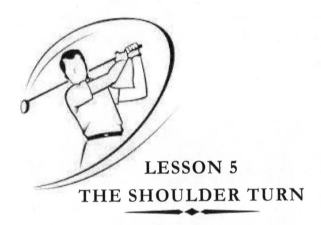

LESSON 5
THE SHOULDER TURN

Every person reading this book, no matter how weak or strong, could have completed the lessons so far. But from half way back to the top a good swing becomes a more athletic move as the top half of the body winds up against the lower half. We're not talking world gymnastic championships but a degree of athleticism is required at this point to maintain your swing arc as the spring is wound up.

Although we haven't discussed it so far in the book, width is important in the golf swing and it is the quality of your shoulder turn that helps maintain the width you created in your stance. At address the left arm is straight and for consistent ball striking it needs to remain relatively straight during the backswing. If width is maintained, not only is the golfer creating maximum potential energy, but a wide arc means the club stays in contact with the ball for the longest possible time through impact— compression rather than a glancing blow.

Without a good shoulder turn width is inevitably lost. If the body stops turning and blocks the arms from swinging freely to the top

two things happen. As the left arm impacts against the chest it starts to bend and automatically swing width is lost. That in itself makes it more difficult to hit the ball consistently but even more damaging is when the arms start to lift up steeply because there is no space for them to travel on the inside. 'Lifting' creates a narrow weak position at the top and makes a solid strike of the ball almost impossible.

Every golfer needs to practise their shoulder turn and following is a great exercise to build up your tummy muscles and core strength so a good turn becomes easy.

Golf Exercise for Shoulder Turn

Throughout this book there is only one piece of equipment I suggest you buy—that's an exercise band, which you can buy from any sports shop. Don't get one with too much tension; buy the one that offers the smallest amount of resistance. If you're a man reading this and feel you might 'bottle' it when asking for the woman's strength exercise band, ask your wife or a friend to buy it. If you buy a band with too much tension the exercise is ruined. This is not a time to be 'macho!'

When you're back home in the garden take the band, a seven iron and take up your stance over an imaginary ball. Hold one end of the band round the grip with you right hand and slip the other end underneath your right foot. The band should have enough slack in it so you can complete a one piece takeaway without it stretching at all. Only when the wrists have hinged should you feel any tension. As you complete the backswing your arms are not strong enough to stretch the band easily on their own and your shoulders have to help out by turning. There should be a constant increase to the tension—no sudden jerky moves.

This exercise leads to an efficient backswing on the right line with the correct width. Your shoulders will have turned correctly and your arms will have stretched into a powerful position at the top. This exercise is a great way to build up the muscles needed to play golf well.

LESSON 6
TOP OF THE BACKSWING

The number one priority of this book was getting you to the top of the backswing in a good position. With the correct grip and stance you now take the club back on the right path. Your wrists now hinge the club perfectly into plane with the butt pointing at the ball. With a good shoulder turn your arms have had enough space to swing to the top maintaining swing width. Wow –you're now in a great position to hit the ball powerfully and accurately. Well done — fantastic work!

But no matter how good a golfer is there is no-one who swings the club into the perfect position every time — there is always something slightly out of place. And it's at the top of the backswing, while the swing is changing direction you have the best chance to find out if anything has gone wrong.

At the top of the backswing, as the club almost comes to a halt, your hands talk to your body and give it feedback about the position the club is in. They let the body know about the line of swing, or in simple terms where the club is aiming. This is called club head awareness — it's an instinctive ability and my definition of natural talent.

With this feedback from the hands the body then calculates what adjustments are needed to get the club onto the right line for a good

downswing. The more time you give your body to compute these calculations the better chance it has of finding the right swing path at the earliest opportunity. The hands of a pro, who point the club accurately at the target don't have much information to pass on except, 'Good to Go' and the downswing can start almost immediately.

But the hands of a high handicap golfer, who is probably pointing the club way off target have so much information to pass on the start of the downswing has to be delayed as the body works out how to try to get the club back into the correct position. The more inexperienced a golfer is, the more time they need to give themselves at the top of the swing in the form of a slight pause.

Pausing at the top is often referred to as 'a well timed swing'. Most golfers have heard the expressions; 'give yourself time to hit the ball', 'swing slow from the top', 'good rhythm'. All these saying refer to the control a golfer shows at the start of the downswing. If the downswing starts after the body has had enough time to calculate the information — it becomes a well timed swing. If a golfer rushes from the top and starts down too early it's pretty much game over. Pausing at the top is a great way to maximise the efficiency of a swing.

Count for Better Pause

To help introduce a pause at the top of the backswing try this exercise. Simply count 'one-*and*-two' to yourself during the swing. 'One' is the backswing. 'And' represents the pause at the top. 'Two' is impact. Most inexperienced golfers swing to the rhythm 'one-two', where there is no pause at all. If you can learn to swing to the count of 'one-*and*-two' you will give your body time to work out what it has to do to hit the ball straight.

A pause at the top will also allow you to hit more powerful shots. Most club golfers rush the downswing because they want to hit the ball with power. But 'hitting from the top' actually sacrifices power and following is an example why.

Imagine a Formula I driver, tantamount to a professional golfer, sitting in his car on the grid. The finish line is half a mile straight down the track—his goal is to drive as fast as possible to the line. Knowing how crucial it is for their driver to have the maximum time to accelerate the mechanics take great care to line up the car as accurately as possible—the equivalent of building a great backswing. Confident the car is aimed accurately, as soon as the green light shows, the driver can floor the accelerator just as a professional golfer can start the downswing almost immediately. Both know that being lined up accurately little can go wrong.

But now it's the turn of a less experienced driver, tantamount to a twenty handicap golfer. He lines up on the grid with his car pointing into the barrier bordering the track (a bad backswing). Can the driver in this car accelerate immediately? Absolutely not! If he did he would go crashing into the wall, spinning down the track.

To make the best of a bad job, first he has to calculate where the car is pointing (pause at the top), then he has to give himself time to steer the car straight. If he carries out the manoeuvre slowly and smoothly he is able to steer onto the right line at the earliest opportunity. But if he tries to go too fast, his initial effort will be overdone and he will go snaking down the track sacrificing accuracy and his potential speed.

The great Jack Nicklaus maintained he played his best golf when he swung slow from the top. It took me ages to fully appreciate what he was saying, but in essence a slow start to the downswing gives a golfer more time to find the right line.

When you hit balls or play on the course make sure you take your time at the top with a slight pause, and then build up speed smoothly to a crescendo at the ball. As you improve your swing the time you need to take at the top will decrease, but when building a new swing you need to take your time.

LESSON 7

THE DOWNSWING
ANCHORING THE HEAD

Having learned the importance of not rushing from the top and therefore finding a good swing path at the start of the downswing, it's time to find out how to keep the swing on a good line as it comes into the ball.. At this point it would be very easy for me to get trapped into talking about the complexity of the downswing but I'm not going to do that because it's not all that difficult.

If I gave you a baseball bat and tossed a ball towards you, you wouldn't need to know in detail how to hit the ball. With regards to golf, from a good position at the top of the backswing the downswing should be instinctive and relatively simple—'keep your head still and swing through to a finish,' is all the advice you should need.

It wouldn't be simple if you hadn't taken time to build a better backswing but if everything is looking okay at the top, there are only two things

 to get right for powerful straight hitting. The position of your head and left foot are crucial on the downswing.

These two parts of your body stabilise the swing and keep it on line as your power and speed build up to impact. The luxury you have is that the correct position of the head and left foot can be secured before the swing even starts. Following is an example of why the position of the head is so important.

Imagine I gave you a long bow just like the one Robin Hood used — massive thing maybe five feet tall and I asked you to fire off an arrow at a distant target. To help shoot accurately you might try to plant the bottom of the bow on the ground to hold it firm. Then you would pull back the string and let the arrow go. But what would happen if the top of the bow moved as you fired off the shot — the arrow would definitely miss the target. In the same way anchoring the head in position during the downswing keeps the swing on line.

Depending on whether you hook or slice you can even select a head position when you set up to the ball that will help control the flight of your shots. If you slice it means your shoulders spin open too much during the downswing. As they spin open they pull the head off its axis. Something has to stop this destructive move, and it's done by setting the head slightly more to the right than normal. This position effectively anchors the top half from spinning open. The opposite head position applies for someone who hooks the ball.

To make sure your head is set at the correct angle carry out this simple test. When you take up your stance (as a right handed golfer) close your left eye. Not only will you see the ball out of your right eye but also the end of your nose. There will be a gap between your nose and the ball. Now slowly tilt *the top* of your head to the right and you will see that gap become smaller. If you want to stop slicing keep your head at this angle. Conversely, if you have a hook and want to attack the ball less from the inside make the gap larger. Experiment with different head positions to see what happens to the ball.

One word of warning—it's no good setting the head at a good angle then allowing it to change during the swing. Your head should maintain the angle you set at address when the swing starts, when you reach the top of the backswing and crucially when the downswing starts. Maintaining a consistent head angle is as important for hitting straight golf shots as keeping the top of the bow still when trying to shoot an arrow.

LESSON 8
ANCHORING THE BOTTOM HALF OF THE BODY

Just as the top half of the body needs to be anchored so does the bottom half. There is an expression in golf you might have heard before—'hitting against a firm left side'. This is to do with getting centrifugal force to release the club naturally into the ball, rather than us having to guide it which we're not very good at. It took me awhile to fully understand the importance of this, so to make it clear I'm going to give you another example.

Imagine an old derelict house that needs to be knocked down—the walls are demolished by a crane arm swinging a heavy ball on the end of a chain. We've all seen it on the TV and the golf swing works in exactly the same way.

So let's look at what happens when the crane tries to knock the wall down. Picture the crane arm with the ball hanging beneath it. To start the ball swinging, the crane arm moves back sweeping the heavy ball away. Once enough momentum has built up the arm of the crane stops allowing the ball to swing past.

When the chain is stretched to its maximum, the arm of the crane starts to move back towards the wall pulling the heavy ball. Then, as the arm of the crane reaches its original position, it comes to an abrupt stop. At this moment centrifugal force kicks in and the ball accelerates past the arm at maximum speed, smashes into the wall and demolishes the house.

Now let's see how this action equates to the golf swing. From your set up position the body turns and swings the club back, just as the crane arm pulls back the chain. Once the swinging motion of the takeaway has built up speed, half way back the right leg resists and the shoulders and arms swing past and stretch to the top of the backswing, just as the crane arm stops and the chain swings past and stretches to its maximum.

On the golf downswing the body unwinds at a smooth constant speed, just as the crane arm moves back towards the wall. But as the body reaches the position it was in at set up, where the shoulders are square, it should stop, just as the arm of the crane stops.

At this moment centrifugal force kicks in and the golf club is literally slung past the body at maximum speed right into the back of the ball, just as the heavy ball smashes into the wall. Being able to hit against a firm left side is crucial

for a powerful accurate release and it can be achieved when you take up your stance.

How to Brace the Left Side

The two main ingredients in a golf swing that enable a golfer to hit against a firm left side are the positions of the head and the left foot. We already know the head should be set slightly back to anchor the top half of the body. Now we have to anchor the left leg.

To make sure the left leg holds firm during the downswing and offers something to hit against, the left foot must be set at the correct angle in the address position. If it's turned towards the target too much there is nothing to stop the hips and shoulders from spinning open out of control. If that happens the club is never able to catch up and it results in a cutting action across the ball.

To stop this from happening the left foot must be set almost at right angles to the target with your body weight importantly set on the inside of the foot. In the same way you need to maintain the head angle until impact, so your weight should stay on the inside of the left foot until you hit the ball. If a golfer allows their weight to crumble onto the outside of the foot during the downswing, stability in the hips is lost and it's all too easy for the shoulders to spin open.

These small adjustments can have a dramatic effect on the efficiency of your downswing. If you have any friends that slice the ball take a moment to think what happens to their left foot when they hit the ball. Even with spikes on their left foot spins open sometimes even tearing grass out. They can even finish with their left foot pointing toward the target. This is the finish position of someone who has completely lost control of their body of the downswing—neither their head nor left leg was sufficiently anchored. If there is nothing to hit against the club will never release.

Here's one last example to hammer home how important it is to anchor the left foot. Imagine you went to the local park and saw a child on one of the swings. As you look closely you see the bolt attaching the swing to the floor is loose. As the child swings forward you can see that the bolt is just about to come out. The whole swing now looks really unstable, shaking about. Maybe it'll even tip over. So you immediately call in the maintenance man. He gets out this great big bolt and hammers it into the ground. There's no way the swing structure will move now. As you watch the child swinging you can see how everything looks more stable.

Setting the left foot firmly into the ground has the same effect of hammering in the bolt. The bottom half of the body must offer resistance for the swinging motion to complete correctly.

Tea and a Chat

By now you know I like to use an analogy to explain something. Well here's one to explain where we are right now with regards to you seeing improvement in your golf. Imagine I took a piece of string, twelve inches long, stretched it out into a straight line and put it on a table. Then two inches to the left I drew a line on the table parallel to it. Six inches to the left of that, the table ends and there's wall. Let's give that wall a name—let's call it the Wall of Patience and Perseverance.

The piece of string is your golf swing. To see a dramatic improvement in the way you hit the ball you have to move all the string over the line. The first thing you try is to get hold of the nearest end and drag it across the table. At first it seems to work and after two inches the end you're holding is over the line. You carry on full of hope and expectation, but six inches later your hand hits the wall—The wall of Patience and Perseverance. Slightly disheartened you start again, but his time further up the piece of string, it's a new theory you've heard about. To start with it looks promising but eventually you hit the wall again. After a few more unsuccessful tries you start to wonder if you'll ever get better.

But then you remember there are two parts to getting the swing right. First of all you have to change your swing path *and then develop a hand action to match it*. Neither one will get the job done on its own. With this new realisation that the swing won't work until both parts complement each other you try a completely new method of moving the string—a two dimensional approach. This time you hold both ends with two hands and start to move it. Moments later the piece of string is completely over the line.

Keep going—we're just about to grab hold of the other end of the string!

LESSON 9
HITTING THROUGH THE SHOT

⬥

Everything we've done so far in this book has pretty much been to do with improving the line of your swing. If I put you on a desert island and got you to hit shots every day, *and you stuck to your new swing with the patience of Job,* there would be no need for me to write the next few chapters. Given time your hands would automatically start to release the club correctly and bring it in square to your new swing path. You are now at exactly the same stage that I was in when I went to play at Effingham Golf Club after my lesson with John Jacobs.

But for two reasons I want to guide you through the last stages. Firstly, you probably haven't got time to hit thousands of balls. Secondly, you might have a swing fault that takes more time to get rid of like a 'chicken wing' left arm. This type of fault occurs when your

swing path travels in one direction and the clubface points radically in another. We now need to synchronise the clubface to your new swing path so at impact you come into the back of the ball and compress it, rather than glancing across it imparting unwanted side spin. It's time to get rid of the residue hanging around from your old action and following is a great exercise to help you do that.

Exercise to Hit Through the Shot Correctly

Take a bucket of balls onto the golf range. Use a seven iron, take up your address and place the clubface right up against the ball so it's touching. Without having any backswing at all, slowly swing the club through to a full finish. If you carry out the action correctly you will almost feel the ball sticking to the clubface before it's slung away ten or fifteen yards up the range. To be able to do this successfully the clubface has to be at right angles to the line of swing through impact.

If the ball immediately slips off it means the face is either open or closed to the swing path. If you suffer from the classic 'chicken wing' left arm, the ball will immediately slip off towards the toe of the club. If you've hooked the ball in the past, and have excessively rolled the hands though impact, the ball will weakly slip off the heel of the club. I must stress at this point how important it is for you to swing through to a full finish every time you try this exercise. Even if the ball slips off immediately — don't quit, carry on to the finish.

Persevere until you can get five consecutive balls into the air. To start with getting even one into the air is difficult. The slower you try this exercise the quicker you will develop a feel for how to get the ball on the club for the longest possible time. At speed this would be called 'compression'. If you manage to start co-ordinating up the clubface with the swing path you will notice that your finish position changes. Someone who has hooked the ball in the past will have more control of the club. The elbows of someone who has habitually sliced will finish up closer together. This is progress and what we're looking for.

LESSON 10

HOLD THE FINISH AND CONTROL THE SWING

I'm sure nearly everyone reading this book will have heard how important it is to finish off the swing in a controlled way. 'Hold your finish' has to be one of the most recognisable expressions in golf. 'FORE' is another that immediately springs to mind. But if holding the finish is so important why do we see so few people doing it. After all, nearly every club golfers has probably tried it at some point. If it really is a useful tip you'd expect to see more people finishing well.

The answer is simple. If a golfer is in the wrong position at the top of the backswing they have to use their body on the way down to try to realign the swing path. If a golfer swings down from a bad position at the top, to a good position on the follow through they would probably miss the ball completely. The golf swing is like an equation—both halves have to match up. To hit the ball straight from a bad backswing, unless your timing is fantastic, you have to have an unbalanced finis. So simply trying to finish nicely is actually counter-productive for most club golfers. They would just turn into great looking hackers.

But after following the lessons in this book you should no longer fit into bracket of 'most club golfers'. You've worked hard to build yourself a

good back swing. You're now one of the few who would benefit on working on a good finish. You might have tried it before—it's time to try it again. If you've practiced the exercise in the previous chapter you should already find that swinging to a well balanced finish is becoming easier. Now I want you to nail it every time.

There are two simple characteristics of a classic finish that that tell a story about the efficiency of the swing. I want you to incorporate both in your finish position.

Two Vital Check Points for a Good Finish

Firstly, your hips should be pointing at the hole—make sure your belt buckle faces the target. This means your body has worked in a co-ordinated way with your hands and arms and has neither been left behind, nor allowed to spin open too much. This sounds really simple but it's not. The hips of someone who habitually slices will tend to have their belt buckle aiming left of target. Someone who normally hooks will have held the hips back at impact and their buckle will point to the right of target. If someone shot a bullet out of your tummy button—it should hit the flag.

Secondly, to make sure you have the correct weight transference for crisp iron shots, make sure your right heel is off the ground (if you are a right handed golfer) with the sole vertical and pointing away from the target. Not to the left – not to the right—directly away from the flag.

This is the classic finish position and if you can to hold it until the ball lands, even if you make slight mistakes during the swing, a well balanced finish will often save the shot from disaster. This will only work for people who have a reasonable backswing or who have such a well timed swing from the top they are able to find the correct swing path at the beginning of the downswing.

LESSON 11
TRUST THE SWING

This is the last thing I'm going to say about the swing and it's to do with the mental side of playing golf rather than to do with swing mechanics. Even with a great swing, if a golfer loses confidence and 'quits' on the shot—it invites disaster. To take on tough shots successfully a golfer must trust his swing and commit to the shot, just as a Formula 1 driver has to trust his car. Following is the final analogy in this book.

Imagine you are sitting in a Formula 1 car and you have to drive round the track in the fastest possible time. The instructors would tell you that when negotiating a difficult bend you have to keep your foot on the accelerator to use down force to glue the car to the road. If you lose confidence and take your foot off the gas, down force is lost and the car goes spinning off the track.

The problem is it's against human instinct to keep accelerating when fear is telling you to slow down. This is where you have to be courageous—this is where you need 'bottle' or 'guts'. To keep control of the car and stay on the road you *have* to keep your foot down and trust the car. The same principles apply to golf.

When a golfer faces a difficult shot on the course the most logical thing to do is stop accelerating and guide the ball towards the target. But that is the worst thing they can do. As soon as they try to manipulate the club and steer the ball, the natural release you've worked so hard to create is interfered with and both power and accuracy are lost. Effectively your ball will go spinning off the track.

For a golfer to hit consistent good shots under pressure they have to be committed to hitting through the ball positively. When facing a tough shot most pros prefer to hit the ball hard knowing it's the best way to keep the shot straight. The swing we have built for you in this book is designed like a Formula 1 car. It's designed to keep you on track at speed. If you back off and don't trust it, it won't work as effectively as if you swing positively and smoothly to the finish position. Trusting your swing is also the quickest way to develop a hand action that matches the new line of your swing.

Trust your swing—it should now be pretty good!

LESSON 12
PRACTICE IN SLOW MOTION

Well I have to congratulate for getting this far. I can't tell you how much I hope your golf improves. When I first started to write this I used an impersonal form but when I started to read back I realised I wasn't being able to talk to you directly. It's almost as though I've been giving you a private lesson. And all my private lessons finish in the same way! I need to tell you how to practise your new swing for maximum benefit.

Practising the Stance

Putting together the four important aspects of the stance you have learned can be summarised as a 'Set up Routine', and it takes time to develop it so it becomes natural. If it was me—I wouldn't even bother to hit balls until this routine became familiar. To give you a goal, once a ball has been put down and lined up at the target, the rest of the routine should take no more than eight seconds. That's your goal.

Clubface:

1. Go to the range and buy a bucket of 50 balls –no more.

2. Find a bay at the end of the range away from any distractions.

3. Take out a seven iron, select a target and get ready to hit.

4. Look at the clubface and see where it's aiming. If you're not sure whether it's correct put a ball down with a line on it and aim that at the target.

5. Take up your stance again—this time with the face at right angles to the line.

6. Now you have eight seconds!

Grip:

1. Lift up your arms to shoulder height and check you could balance a club on them.

2. If you couldn't, adjust your shoulders and left hand grip, till you can.

3. Drop the arms down and make sure that a line across them would point at the target.

4. Ask a friend to put a club across your forearms if you're not sure.

Legs and Feet:

1. Make sure your legs are set in an athletic position.

2. Imagine if I tried to push you over—are your legs firm enough to resist?

3. Set you left foot almost at right angles to the hole.

4. Make sure that your body weight is on the inside of both feet.

Head Position:

1. Close your left eye to see the gap between your nose and the ball.

2. If you normally slice narrow the gap by tilting the top of your head to the right.

3. If you tend to hook the ball make the gap larger by tilting your head to the left.

4. Keep it at the same angle till you've hit the ball.

    The more you practise this routine the easier the next part of the swing becomes.

The Swing—Practising a One Piece takeaway

1. Take up your stance and pull the club up through your hands till the butt touches your belt buckle.

2. Slowly swing back and forward using only your body—no hands at all!

3. Swing no more than two feet either way and keep the triangle together throughout.

4. Once this pendulum action feels familiar, put a ball on a short tee, hold the club correctly and gently clip a few balls away keeping the unit solid.

5. Hit the balls no more than fifteen yards — effectively you're practising a chipping action.

6. Do this until the ball start comes out of the middle of the club and goes dead straight.

7. Keep the swing short both ways.

8. Even though it's a small swing, make sure you keep the head position you set constant throughout.

9. Keeping the head still on this short shot starts to educate the body how it should work on the downswing when you build up to full power.

Wrist Cock

1. Swing back using your one piece takeaway.

2. When you've swung back a few feet cock the wrists and point the butt of the club at the ball. As your confidence increases you should feel your wrists starting to hinge naturally.

3. After practising a few swings try hitting a few shots off a tee.

4. Say to yourself, 'turn — point — hit'.

5. Make sure you swing through the same distance as you swing back.

6. In the finish position of the half swing, the butt of the club should point back at where the ball was on the tee.

7. Although the two halves of the swing should be mirror images with regards to line and plane, even though it's a short follow through make sure your right foot comes up into the classic position.

8. If you top the ball to begin with, change your saying to 'turn — point — right foot up', as this helps to make sure you transfer your weight forward during the swing.

Full Swing

1. Do some slow motion practise swings first.

2. Remember the full swing requires some effort to continue turning the shoulders from half way back.

3. If you swing in slow motion you will be able to say the following words to yourself, as you carry out the movements. 'Turn the body — point the butt at the

ball—stretch to the top—head back—
right foot up in the finish'.

4. Each slow motion swing might take a few
    seconds for you to complete.

5. As you get used to the 'feel' reduce your
    saying to, 'turn—point—stretch—head—
    finish'.

6. As you further increase speed the wrists
    should start to hinge naturally and you
    can reduce your saying to 'turn—
    stretch—head—finish'.

7. When you finally swing at normal speed
    reduce the saying to 'turn—head—finish'.
    Or you can substitute naming the
    individual movements for 'one—and—
    two'.

You've now got all the information you need to
improve your golf swing and it's not just a
question of hitting lots of balls. Unless you
practise with a goal in mind you're wasting time.
Chose any of the points I have listed in this book,
go away and patiently try to groove it. It doesn't
really matter which part it is. Remember, the golf
swing is a chain reaction—get any section right
and the part after and even before will become
easier.

Incredible—well done! Don't expect miracles to
begin with—remember how I wasted ten years
not being patient enough to allow the changes to
work. But great stuff—kudos to you!

SO LONG...FOR NOW

Well it's time to say goodbye or more appropriately *hasta la vista* as I'm writing this book in Spain. I don't know if you've ever written a book before but it's quite an emotional experience and quite a commitment. Last night at two in the morning I was standing in front of the mirror pretending I was passing a bucket of water to someone making sure the example I gave of the takeaway 'feel' was correct!

They say you have to spend 10,000 hours practising a skill before you can call yourself an expert. Well, times that by seven and you get close to how many hours I have spent studying and practising the golf swing. I've hit over 2,000,000 balls and have tried every conceivable technique and swing tip. Had I written a golf instruction book twenty years ago it would have been about three hundred pages long, but now, with all my experience, I've been able to condense that information into about thirty.

Some of the purists might criticise a few expressions I've used in the book. A scientist might point out that it's, 'centripetal force' that is used in the golf swing, not centrifugal force as I have referred to. But hey—the difference is so minimal it would only lead to confusion.

As you've read this far you know I like a good analogy. Well here's my very last one. You know kids and their computers? Sometimes they play an adventure game where the hero has to find weapons to kill the dragon that's terrorising the local village. As they start the game they have two options. They can go straight to the shops on the left and buy the most expensive looking sword they can afford. Or they can walk over the small bridge to speak to the little man standing in the shade. Most kids go straight to the shops. But if they took time to speak to the little man, they'd find he has a nugget of information he can pass on. He can tell you exactly how to kill the dragon and it's not with the sword or the latest golf clubs on sale.

In the same way there are two options now open to you now. You could go out and buy expensive clubs, spend money on lessons, or even employ a top sports psychologist in your search to play better golf. On the other hand you could simply take the advice I offer in this book. The information on these pages is born from thousands of hours practising my trade. All you need to transform your game is patience and a realisation that things might not get better straight away — change takes time.

I'm sure some of you will be asking the question, 'well if he knows so much why haven't we heard of him'. It's a good question. Two things have happened in my life that have halted my progress as a player — firstly injury. In 1985 I hurt my leg which put paid to that season. Ironically it was the season the European Tour became all exempt and I missed out of getting my tour card by a few hundred pounds. But worse — far worse, in 1994 I made a mistake that had tragic and devastating consequences.

I've written three books in total — they're not all about golf. My first book is about a journey I once faced which I hope you never have to undertake. It's called 'Inside — One Mans Experience of Prison'. It'll shock you if you read it — it's available most everywhere ebooks are sold. It certainly shocks the many youngsters I work with when I'm not teaching golf. But it's meant to shock — that's the point of the book.

But back to golf. Remember how much time I wasted because I didn't persevere with the advice John Jacobs gave to me when I was a young man. If you've enjoyed this book — or at least found it interesting, please do try to stick to the lessons I've laid down. Work through them slowly with patience and don't judge them on whether you get immediate results.

Finally, this is not goodbye—more *adieu*. If you get stuck or don't understand something, write to me and I will reply. You will find my email address at the very end of this book. I wish you luck—it's been a privilege.

ALSO...
BY JOHN HOSKISON

INSIDE
One Man's Experience of Prison
A True Story

NAME AND NUMBER:
Based On a True Prison Story

LOWER YOUR GOLF SCORE:
Simple Steps to Save Shots

YOUR SHORT GAME SILVER BULLET
Golf Swing Drills for Club Head Control

John Hoskison was educated at St John's Leatherhead. After a short time working in a bank, he became a professional golfer and played the European PGA tour until 1985.

Elected Surrey Professional Golf Association Captain, John and has twice represented Europe in PGA Cup matches against America. He has also led England in the European Team Championships.

In 1992, he won the Club Professionals Grand Slam including the national title.

After ten years speaking at schools and universities about his experiences in prison, John competed in the qualifying school to gain a place on the European PGA Seniors Tour. He was successful and out of an original field of 300 he finished second. In May 2008 he played in his first event in Poland.

Currently, John spends time competing at golf, writing articles for an international sports magazine and speaking at schools about facing adversity and the importance of being able to say 'no'. He has now spoken at over 300 schools to over 40,000 pupils.

If you wish to contact John directly, please email Hoskison51@hotmail.com. Or you may contact John through his publisher at jHoskison@epublishingworks.com